Anne Hutchinson

Susan Bivin Aller

BARNES & NOBLE

NEW YORK

Text © 2010 by Susan Bivin Aller
Illustrations © 2010 by Lerner Publishing Group, Inc.

This 2010 edition published by Barnes & Noble, Inc.
by arrangement with Lerner Publications Company, a division of
Lerner Publishing Group, Inc., Minneapolis, MN.

Illustrations by Tad Butler

ISBN-13: 978-1-4351-1896-6

Printed and bound in the United States of America

1 - VI - 12/15/2009

The quotes in this book have been drawn from many sources, and are assumed to be accurate as quoted
in their previously published forms. Although every effort has been made to verify the quotes and sources,
the publishers cannot guarantee their perfect accuracy.

All Web sites and URLs in this book are current at the point of publication. However, Web sites may be
taken down and URLs may change after publication without notice. The Publisher and the Author are
not responsible for the content contained in any specific Web site featured in this book, nor shall they be
liable for any loss or damage arising from the information contained in this book.

TABLE OF CONTENTS

INTRODUCTION

Anne Marbury Hutchinson lived in Boston, Massachusetts, in the 1600s. She belonged to a group of Christians called Puritans. Anne believed that God spoke to her through the Bible. She felt this important book guided her life. She believed God spoke to her directly too. She held meetings at her house to explain the Bible and to talk about God's messages.

In 1637, leaders from Anne's church put her on trial. They said she was teaching false ideas. The judges found Anne guilty. She could no longer be a member of the church. They made her leave the Massachusetts Bay Colony.

Anne was a brave woman. She stood up for her right to speak about what she believed. In doing so, she lost her home, her church, and finally her life.

This is her story.

1 DAUGHTER OF A PREACHER

Anne Marbury was born in the town of Alford, England, in 1591. At that time, there were two main Christian religions in England. One was the Church of England. The other was the Roman Catholic Church.

Sixty years before Anne was born, most people in England were Catholic. Then King Henry VIII broke away from the Roman Catholic Church. He created the Church of England and made himself the head of it. The Church of England was part of a movement called Protestantism. Protestants disagreed with or protested many Catholic beliefs and practices.

Churchgoers attend a Protestant service in England.

Eleven years after Henry died, his daughter Elizabeth became queen. Queen Elizabeth I continued Henry's work. Catholic decorations, such as statues and stained glass windows, were taken out of English churches. Church of England Protestants were taught to read their Bibles and pray directly to God. Catholics instead went to their priests to hear what God wanted them to do.

Queen Elizabeth I continued to support Protestantism as England's main religion.

A Puritan family sits down to dinner. Puritans wore plain clothing and led simple lives.

Anne's parents belonged to the Church of England. They were members of a group within the church called Puritans. Puritans wanted to purify, or free, the church of all Catholic traditions. For example, Puritans didn't celebrate saints' days and holy days.

This painting from the 1600s pictures a Puritan meeting (church service).

Puritans also did not kneel in church or make the sign of the cross before praying. Their ministers wore plain black robes.

Puritans disagreed with church officials who gave preaching jobs to poorly educated men. The Puritans said ministers should be educated. They should fully understand the Bible. Puritans believed it was the job of ministers to preach powerful, intelligent sermons.

Anne's father, Francis Marbury, was a Protestant minister. He had a degree from Cambridge, one of England's best universities. Twelve years before Anne was born, he had been put in prison for disagreeing with church leaders. When Anne was born, he was in trouble again for the same crime. He was not allowed to preach.

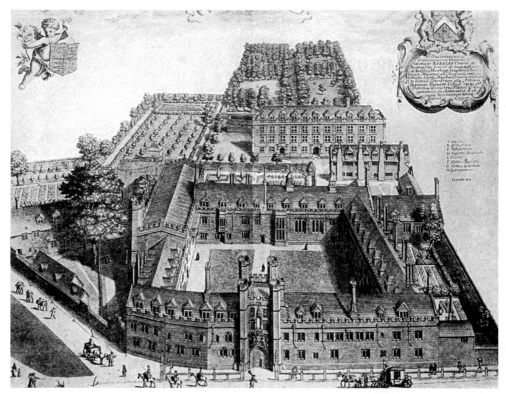

Anne's father, Francis Marbury, attended Cambridge University.

Marbury was also a schoolmaster. His trouble with church leaders stopped him from teaching. But he and Anne's mother, Bridget, taught their fifteen children at home. At the time, girls weren't allowed to go to school. But all the Marbury girls and boys learned to read and write. Anne was the smartest of all. She memorized Bible verses almost as soon as she could talk.

Anne's mother also taught her how to be a nurse and midwife. A midwife helps women during childbirth.

A Puritan woman reads the Bible as she spins wool into yarn.

When Anne was fourteen, church officials allowed her father to preach and to teach school again. He had promised to stop criticizing the Church of England. In October 1605, he was sent to the church of St. Martin in the Vintry in London, England's capital.

THE GUNPOWDER PLOT

Puritans tried to remove all traces of Catholicism from the Church of England. Many Catholics felt under attack and fought back. A secret group of Catholics hid thirty-six barrels of gunpowder under the building where government leaders met. They planned to blow it up when the king and other leaders arrived. On November 5, 1605, the Gunpowder Plot was uncovered.

In modern England, people celebrate the Fifth of November with bonfires and fireworks. They also burn a stuffed dummy called Guy. The dummy is named for Guy Fawkes, the Catholic man caught guarding the gunpowder.

The Marburys' new house stood close to the Tower of London and the Thames River. Large audiences watched the plays of William Shakespeare at Bankside, just across the river. London must have seemed noisy, crowded, and exciting to Anne after her early years in a small country town.

This illustration shows what London looked like in the 1500s. The Thames River (BOTTOM) flows past Saint Paul's Cathedral in central London.

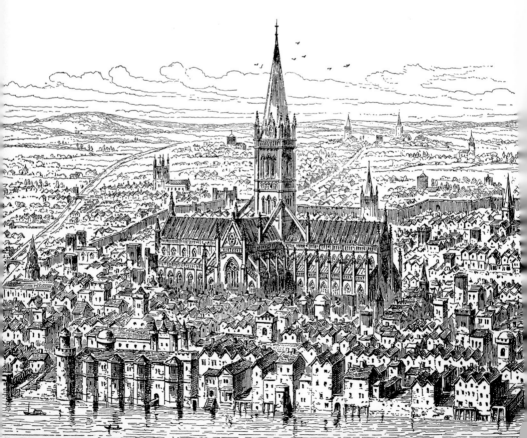

2 AMERICAN PURITAN

Anne married William Hutchinson in 1612, when she was twenty-one. Hutchinson was a Puritan merchant who bought and sold wool. He and Anne had known each other in Alford. They saw each other when he traveled to London on business. After their marriage, the couple moved back to their hometown to start a family.

A Puritan man and woman exchange marriage vows in front of a Puritan minister.

Anne Hutchinson's first child was born nine months after her wedding. She had a baby every year or two until she was forty-two years old. In all, she had fifteen babies. That number was not unusual then. But it was unusual that all fifteen Hutchinson children lived. In the 1600s, about half of all children died before the age of three. One in five mothers died in childbirth.

Anne was often called to help someone who was sick or having a baby. Other women went with her to help. They worked long hours or sometimes days. During these times, Anne shared what she knew about the Bible. Many of the women could not read or write. They were not allowed to speak in church or ask questions of ministers. But they trusted Anne and found it easy to talk to her.

A midwife (RIGHT) helps a pregnant woman (CENTER) give birth. Anne served as a nurse and midwife to her friends and neighbors.

In 1634, Anne, William, and their children sailed from England to America. They left because they were afraid that King Charles I was trying to get rid of the Puritans. Four years earlier, a group of nearly one thousand Puritans had left England for the New World. They settled in the new colony of Massachusetts Bay. They began building a city named Boston.

PURITAN OR PILGRIM?

A group of English people known as the Pilgrims were early settlers in America. They sailed on the *Mayflower* in 1620 and built Plymouth (or Plimouth) Plantation in Massachusetts. But were the Pilgrims and Puritans the same? The Pilgrims were a small group of Puritans called Separatists. They wanted to break away, or separate, from England entirely. One of their leaders, William Bradford, first called the group Pilgrims. A pilgrim is someone who travels to foreign lands.

These houses were built to look like the houses in Boston at the time Anne lived there. Anne's house was much larger.

The Hutchinsons' ship landed in Boston Harbor. Beyond the harbor, Anne saw a great flat marsh with a few groups of buildings. Anne said her heart sank at the sight. In 1634, Boston's eight hundred settlers lived mainly in huts with thatched straw roofs. Only a few rich people had solid houses.

This illustration shows a Puritan minister and his followers in the Massachusetts Bay Colony.

William Hutchinson had become a rich man. He bought a piece of land and built one of the largest houses in Boston for Anne and his children.

One of their neighbors was the most powerful man in Massachusetts, John Winthrop. He was governor of the colony. He had come from Norfolk, England, four years earlier, leading eleven ships full of Puritans. He was a proud lawyer who was trusted for his honesty. He worked hard to make the colony do well.

The most important organization in Boston was the church. Anne's friend John Cotton was its preacher. Anne had attended his church back in England, in a town also called Boston. Cotton had left England because the church court thought he was teaching false ideas. He had moved to the new Boston in America to escape punishment.

John Cotton preached in the Puritan church in Boston, Massachusetts.

A man could not vote or take part in business in the colony if he didn't belong to the Boston church. Colony leaders questioned Anne and William when they arrived to be sure they believed and understood Puritan ideas. Then they were allowed to join the church. John Cotton gladly welcomed Anne. She had been one of his most helpful church members in England.

The first Puritans in Boston held church meetings in this building.

3 TEACHER AND PROPHET

Anne and William quickly became leaders in the colony. William joined the General Court, the group of men who made laws and decided punishments. Anne helped others as a nurse and midwife.

Many neighbors came to hear Anne (LEFT) preach in her home.

She also spoke to women about their religion. She encouraged them to talk about their belief in God and to ask questions. Preaching and Bible study were very important to Puritans. So Anne's teachings made her one of the most respected women in the colony.

At that time, many women could not go to church because they had so much to do at home. Anne began to hold weekly meetings in her house for them. She talked about the Sunday sermon and added her own ideas. More women came. Anne added a second weekly meeting. Some husbands became curious. They began to come to the meetings too.

Then Governor Henry Vane started coming. Vane was only twenty-three years old. He had won an election against John Winthrop just a few months after arriving in the colony in 1636.

Vane was handsome and smart. He belonged to an important English family. His father was an adviser to the king.

Vane rented rooms at John Cotton's house. It was there that he heard about Anne. When he started going to Anne's meetings, he made them even more popular. People crowded into the Hutchinson house. Sometimes sixty or eighty were there at a time.

Henry Vane attended Anne's weekly meetings.

25

Anne told her followers that God spoke to her and gave her messages. This made the colony's preachers angry. They said that all of God's messages were written in the Bible. God was not giving any new ones, especially not to a woman like Anne! Everyone agreed the Bible had all the rules for leading a good life. But the preachers said that only they had the training to explain the Bible to others. They did not want people learning wrong things about God and the Bible.

Preachers were also afraid that if people listened to Anne, the preachers might not be needed as much. The preachers were a powerful group in the colony. They didn't want to lose their control.

Puritans attend a church service in Massachusetts. Many preachers did not like Anne holding meetings in her home.

New England Puritans believed they were living in the final days of the world. They believed that God would soon come and take the people he had chosen to heaven. Puritans also believed that God had already decided who these people were. This teaching was called predestination.

NEEDING HARVARD

In 1637, the General Court started a college to train ministers. It was in Newtown (later called Cambridge), Massachusetts. They named the college Harvard, after the Reverend John Harvard. John Harvard left a gift of money and books to the new school.

Harvard College's mission was to educate a new group of preachers who agreed on religious ideas. The General Court hoped that this would stop the colonists from disagreeing about religious ideas in the future.

People were very worried about whether they were chosen. Anne told them how they could find out. She said people should pray, admit their sins, and study the Bible carefully. After awhile, people would feel the Holy Spirit (a part of God) move inside them. Feeling the Holy Spirit was considered a gift from God. He gave them the gift to show that he had chosen them. Anne said people didn't have to do good works to earn this gift. Most of the colony's ministers disagreed with Anne.

By the spring of 1637, arguments about religion were splitting the colony apart. Leaders were afraid that the king might send a royal governor to stop the trouble and run the colony. Massachusetts wanted to remain separate from England. The only way to do that was to get rid of the troublemakers. The General Court had to silence Anne.

4 "ROOT OF ALL THE MISCHIEF"

In May 1637, John Winthrop and the General Court called for an election. They wanted to vote Henry Vane out of the job as governor because he supported Anne Hutchinson. Winthrop wrote that the men at this meeting made "fierce speeches" and even began to fight. Finally, one preacher climbed a tree. He demanded the vote be taken. Vane lost the election. Winthrop became governor again.

Governor Winthrop called a meeting to discuss Anne's actions.

Governor Winthrop then called for a synod of all the colony's churches. A synod is a formal meeting to settle problems. Members of the synod met in Newtown, outside Boston, for more than three weeks. They wanted to charge Anne with eighty-two charges of teaching "errors" to her followers.

Anne probably went to the synod. But as a woman, she wouldn't have been allowed to speak. Her heart must have pounded when she heard the men say that her house meetings were against the law. She would be put on trial.

On a freezing day in November 1637, the General Court met in the Newtown meetinghouse. Anne's trial began. The room was packed with men wearing black hats and heavy winter cloaks. At the front, forty judges of the General Court sat on long wooden benches facing the crowd. Eight church ministers in black robes joined them.

The General Court upheld Puritan laws. In this image, a man is being held in stocks. Stocks were wooden devices used to punish people in public.

Everyone turned to see Anne enter the meetinghouse with her husband and other family members. Anne was forty-six years old and pregnant for the sixteenth time. She wore a white cap and a long wool cloak. Many of the men knew Anne well. She had nursed their wives and children. Even John Winthrop had been her neighbor for years. She had just taken care of Winthrop's wife, who was still in bed after losing a baby in childbirth.

This sketch of Anne wearing traditional Puritan dress was made during her lifetime.

Anne stands before the court.

Winthrop called Anne to come forward. She was not allowed to have a lawyer. She walked alone to the front and stood before her judges.

Winthrop described Anne as "haughty" (proud and vain). He said she had "a very voluble tongue." That meant she talked too much. Winthrop didn't like educated women. He thought too much reading and writing were bad for them. And he believed Anne led women to spend too much time away from their families.

Winthrop stated the charges against her. Anne, he said, had troubled the peace of the colony. She had been holding large meetings in her home. And she had criticized the ministers.

Anne said that none of these activities was against the law. She did not understand what she did wrong. The governor pushed on. He and his fellow judges, he said, needed to "take such course that you may trouble us no further."

The trial lasted for two days. Preachers and judges argued on one side. Anne argued brilliantly on the other.

QUAKERS IN THE COLONY

Anne believed that God sends the Holy Spirit to people to guide them. That belief is closely related to Quaker teachings. The Quakers also came to America from England. Quakers who disagreed with the Puritans were put on trial, as Anne was. One of Anne's followers, Mary Dyer, became a Quaker. She was later hanged in Boston for her beliefs.

But the judges held the most power. They wanted to find her guilty. Near the end of the second day, Anne knew she was losing. She tried to stand up for her right to preach what she believed. She shocked the court by saying God spoke directly to her and told her what the future held. She said that if the ministers and judges did not change their ways, they would be cursed. She herself would have many troubles, but God would take care of her.

Some Puritans defended Anne. In this illustration, colonist William Coddington (CENTER) argues to end Anne's trial.

Anne's claims about God talking to her angered Governor Winthrop. "This is the thing," he declared, "that [has] been the root of all the mischief."

Winthrop called for a vote. The court voted to arrest Anne. She could stay under arrest in her home during the long, hard winter. Then she would have to leave Massachusetts.

"I desire to know wherefore [why] I am banished," Anne demanded.

"The court knows wherefore," answered Winthrop, "and is satisfied."

5 IN THE WILDERNESS

While under arrest, Anne still had many visitors. She still spoke about messages from God. Ministers went to see her to discuss her ideas. But they were not really interested. Instead, they trapped her into making even more "errors," as they called them. They made a long list of these errors. The Boston church decided to try Anne in court again. This time the charge was heresy, or false religious beliefs.

In March 1638, the court met in Boston to finish their business with Anne. John Cotton tried to help. But she refused to back down on her beliefs. At last, the judges took away her membership in the church. She was also accused of lying. They ordered her to leave the colony by the end of March.

Anne, her husband, and their younger children went to Rhode Island. They set up the town of Portsmouth with other people who had left Massachusetts for religious reasons. That summer, Anne's sixteenth pregnancy ended sadly. The baby did not live. Many people thought this was a punishment for Anne's sins.

This Puritan family was banished from Massachusetts. Anne and her family had to leave their home too.

This illustration shows Rhode Island as it appeared in 1638, the year Anne and her family moved there.

Anne still attracted followers and held meetings in Rhode Island. She taught both men and women. Once, an earthquake struck during a prayer meeting. She announced the Holy Spirit was coming down on them. She felt this was a special message from God. She wrote to the Boston church and told them she had been given a message that they would be destroyed.

Anne's husband died in 1642. At the same time, Anne feared that Massachusetts would take over the Rhode Island colony. If that happened, she would be jailed or even killed. She knew she had to move. She told her family that God had made a safe place for her in the Dutch settlement of New Amsterdam (later called New York). She bought farmland in Pelham, in what later became the Bronx, New York City.

Anne bought land from the Dutch in New Amsterdam (ABOVE). She moved her family there in 1642.

Anne gathered her children, farm animals, and all that she owned. They moved once more to a new land. She was warned of the danger of attacks by Native Americans. But Anne felt protected by God. She had always opposed making slaves of Native Americans or taking their lands by war. She had lived near them safely in Massachusetts and Rhode Island. "We are all one Indian," she said.

This illustration shows a Puritan family protecting themselves against an attack by Native Americans.

Siwanoy warriors attacked Anne and her family in 1643.

The Dutch and Native Americans had been at war in New Amsterdam for several years. Surprise attacks from both sides were common. In late summer 1643, a group of Native Americans called the Siwanoy stormed toward Anne's settlement. Most settlers fled to the Dutch military fort. But Anne, her family, and her followers stayed on their land.

The Siwanoy warriors attacked. They killed Anne and six of her children. One young Hutchinson daughter lived. She was captured and stayed with the Siwanoy for several years before being let go.

Anne Hutchinson led a full life as "wife, mother, midwife, . . . and spiritual leader." These words are on a monument in Portsmouth, Rhode Island. She was one of the earliest American women who had the courage to stand up for her right to speak about what she believed.

ANNE'S DESCENDANTS

At the time of her death, Anne had twelve living children. Only seven of the youngest went with her to New Amsterdam. When the Siwanoy attacked, six of them were killed.

Her older surviving children married and had many descendants. These include Massachusetts and Rhode Island governors and three U.S. presidents (Franklin D. Roosevelt, George H. W. Bush, and George W. Bush).

TIMELINE

ANNE MARBURY HUTCHINSON WAS BORN ON JULY 17, 1591, IN ALFORD, ENGLAND.

In the year...

1605   Anne's family moves to London.   Age 14

1611   Anne's father dies.

1612   Anne marries William Hutchinson, a wool   Age 21
merchant.

     They move back to Alford.

1613   The first of Anne's fifteen children is born.

1630   John Winthrop leads English Puritans to the
Massachusetts Bay Colony.

1633   Reverend John Cotton goes to Boston,
Massachusetts, to escape punishment in
England.

1634   Anne and her family move to Boston.   Age 43

     She begins her home discussion groups for
women.

1636   Governor Henry Vane becomes a follower
of Anne.

1637   Anne is tried and sentenced to house arrest   Age 46
in November.

1638   Anne is found guilty in a second trial.

     She is cut off from her church and has to
leave the colony.

     She and her family move to Rhode Island.

1642   Anne's husband dies.

     She moves her family to Dutch lands in
Pelham, New York.

1643   Anne and her children are killed by Native   Age 52
American warriors.

REMEMBERING ANNE

In Boston, Massachusetts, a bronze statue of Anne Hutchinson with her young daughter *(below)* stands on the lawn in front of the State House. The Hutchinsons' house at the corner of Washington and School streets burned down in 1711. In 1718, a brick building called the Old Corner Book Store was built on the same spot.

In Portsmouth, Rhode Island, a plaque in the Anne M. Hutchinson Memorial Park (or Founders Brook Park) honors Anne as an original settler of Portsmouth in 1638.

Some artifacts that were uncovered at the site of her house are on display at the Portsmouth Public Library.

In New York, lasting tributes to Anne are found in the names of the Hutchinson River, the Hutchinson River Parkway, and numerous schools in New York and elsewhere.

FURTHER READING

Collier, Christopher, and James Lincoln Collier. *Pilgrims and Puritans: 1620–1676.* New York: Benchmark Books, 1998. The Colliers explain the politics and religion of America's early European settlers and the hardships they faced.

Hinman, Bonnie. *The Massachusetts Bay Colony.* Hockessin, DE: Mitchell Lane, 2007. English Puritans came to the Massachusetts Bay Colony in search of religious freedom. Read how the colony became an important part of the founding of a new country.

Miller, Brandon Marie. *Growing Up in a New World: 1607 to 1775.* Minneapolis: Lerner Publications Company, 2003. Miller takes a detailed look at what it was like to be a child or young adult in colonial America.

Slavicek, Louise Chipley. *Life among the Puritans.* San Diego: Lucent Books, 2001. Learn about Plymouth Colony and the Massachusetts Bay Colony and how the religious beliefs of Puritans and Pilgrims shaped their daily lives.

WEBSITES

History for Kids: Puritans
http://www.historyforkids.org/learn/northamerica/after1500/religion/puritans.htm
Read about the Puritans in North America, with links to other early religious settlers and to Native American groups.

The Puritans
http://www.mce.k12tn.net/colonial_america/puritans.htm
Learn why some settlers left the Massachusetts Bay Colony and settled other colonies in early New England.

SELECT BIBLIOGRAPHY

Ahlstrom, Sydney E. *A Religious History of the American People*. New Haven, CT: Yale University Press, 1972.

La Plante, Eve. *American Jezebel*. New York: HarperCollins, 2004.

Leonardo, Bianca, and Winifred K. Rugg. *Anne Hutchinson: Unsung Heroine of History*. Joshua Tree, CA: Tree of Life Publications, 1995.

Robson, Lloyd A. "Anne Hutchinson and Her Neighbors." Bulletin of the Newport Historical Society, no. 99, August 1938, 22–39.

Staloff, Darren. *The Making of an American Thinking Class*. New York: Oxford University Press, 1998.

Williams, J. Paul. *What Americans Believe and How They Worship*. New York: Harper, 1952.

Winship, Michael P. *The Times and Trials of Anne Hutchinson: Puritans Divided*. Lawrence: University Press of Kansas, 2005.

INDEX

Acknowledgments

For photographs and artwork: © James P. Rowan, p. 4; The Granger Collection, New York, pp. 7, 9, 14, 17, 25, 26, 40, 42; © The Bridgeman Art Library/Getty Images, p. 8; Saltram House, Devon, UK/National Trust Photographic Library/Rob Matheson/The Bridgeman Art Library, p. 10; © Topham/The Image Works, p. 11; © North Wind Picture Archives, pp. 12, 16, 20, 22, 31, 33, 38; © Visual Mining/Alamy, p. 19; © Bettmann/CORBIS, pp. 21, 24, 32; © Stock Montage/Hulton Archive/Getty Images, p. 30; © The New York Public Library/Art Resource, NY, p. 35; © The Image Works Archives, p. 39; © MPI/Hulton Archive/Getty Images, p. 41; © Kevin Fleming/CORBIS, p. 45. Front cover: The Granger Collection, New York. Back cover: © Wikimedia Foundation, Inc./Hi540.
For quoted material: p. 29, Lloyd A. Robson, "Anne Hutchinson and Her Neighbors," Bulletin of the Newport Historical Society, no. 99, August 1938, 28; p. 33, Eve La Plante, *American Jezebel* (New York: HarperCollins, 2004), 3; p. 34, Michael P. Winship, *The Times and Trials of Anne Hutchinson: Puritans Divided* (Lawrence: University Press of Kansas, 2005), 105; p. 36, Ibid., 103; p. 36, Ibid., 114; p. 41, Ibid., 146.